Barry Spacks

TEACHING
THE PENGUINS
TO FLY

DAVID R. GODINE

BOSTON

FOR JUDITH

David R. Godine, Publisher
Boston, Massachusetts

Copyright © 1960, 1972, 1973, 1974, 1975
by Barry Spacks
Title page illustration copyright © 1975 by Judith Spacks

LCC 74-25958
ISBN 0-87923-118-1
Printed in the United States of America

Acknowledgments: 'Globed Thistles' and 'Teaching the Penguins to Fly' first appeared in *The Hudson Review* (Winter 1974-1975). 'To a Lady,' 'Comparing X-Rays,' and 'Recalling Mr. Frost' first appeared in the *New York Times*; copyright 1961, 1972 by The New York Times Company. 'Essential Praises of Silence' first appeared in *The New Yorker*; copyright 1974 by The New Yorker Magazine, Inc. 'A Quiet Day' and 'Before a Statue of Kuan Yin' first appeared in *Poetry*. Other poems first appeared in *The Atlantic Monthly, Bartleby's Review, The Beloit Poetry Journal, The Boston Phoenix, The Carleton Miscellany, Mr. Cogito, Esquire, The Midwest Quarterly, Modern Occasions, The Nation, Outerbridge, Ploughshares, The Sewanee Review, Southern Poetry Review*.

A Godine Poetry Chapbook
Second Series

CONTENTS

I   A Quiet Day   7

Nursing Home   8

On a Photograph by Emmet Gowin   9

My Mother's Childhood   10

The Girl Not Invited   11

Cramps   12

Not Seeing the Sea   13

'Who Then Is Crazy?'   14

The Evidence   15

My Old Professor in a Bar   16

My Teacher   17

Borges in Cambridge   19

II   Little Song   21

Stone Soup   22

Teaching the Penguins to Fly   23

Administrator's Poem   24

John Berryman   25

The Young   27

The Old   28

The Dream Burglar   29

Tombstones & Flourishes   30

Recalling Mr. Frost   31

III   Once the World's On Again   33

'Foolfish'   34

Globed Thistles   35

The Legend of Kuan Yin   36

Before a Statue of Kuan Yin   36

In the Forties   37

Comparing X-Rays   38

Variation on a Theme From Horace   39
Spider   40
To a Lady   41
Song of the Scholar of Love   42
Found Art   43
Essential Praises of Silence   44
After the 'I Ching'   46
On a Jaina Miniature   47
Courting Surfaces   48

Teaching the Penguins to Fly

I

A Quiet Day

My poem, I place the weight of the day
    on your shoulders;
a quiet day, no gong of terror sounding.
Not the grand style of the Hectors striding forth,
but the quiet braveries take you, say the man
unlocking his store at eight despite
the gunmen;
or the feverish child, her parents all night beside her;
or my neighbor McFee, sweat dripping from his chin,
eighty-four and he feels it,
painting his empty home.
Or a wife assisting the long divorce of her husband
from his large dreams. The quiet day
before; the day
just after.

Nursing Home

My mother babbles. A salad of noises.
'You know who this is?' asks my aunt and I dread
some horror of an answer, but no,
nothing. She rubs her tray instead.
'It's clean,' says my aunt, 'the tray is clean.
Evelyn, what are you cleaning? Play
with your cards, play *pishy-posh*,' and then she
laughs, that overflowing, tilts
her head at the word and laughs who sits
all day in her chair with her cards in a sweater
embroidered with flowers, all day each day
where the t.v. flickers. My aunt thinks she chose
senility. My aunt says you have to keep
moving, never worry, avoid
abiding mourning,
things that refuse to change.

On a Photograph by Emmet Gowin

Camera-blurred in the corner an old woman
sits, not attending. A young woman,
angry because she is tired, perhaps,
of sudden photographer's orders (*let's see
those tits*), or angrily proud, taunting
Age and Death, yanks open her sweater
—or is she trying to cover against
the lewdness of the lens?—displaying
her breast, the milk-yielding
human breast.

Proud or shy or petulant,
her anger says that God is male,
and male the lens, and male the thought
that stills her, steals this much of her,
and loves her by consumption.

My Mother's Childhood

When she still used words, my mother told
of her childhood: they were poor, her father
peddled insurance door-to-door
in Portland, where the firehouse bell
would ring *no school* come heavy snow
and she'd stand—her little shrug, her sheepish
grin—in the candy factory yard,
waiting, patient child in the cold,
for sometimes an upper window would open,
someone would throw down gum, lumps
as large as little pumpernickels;
grey, but tasty. How she chewed!
She never wondered then, was it pure?
rejected?—chewed till her jawbones ached
and the tears welled in her eyes—they only
threw to her, to her, because
she waited,
and was good.

The Girl Not Invited

What will sweeten the life of the girl
not invited? There works a bitterness
yellow through gauze, an acid stench
no words diffuse, staining the cells
of her nature. What if everyone
were invited, say for a thousand years,
till even her lump's distinction, her lead-grained
silence leached away, and the starch
of pain had dimmed from the fiber? Who could
like her, want her, dustier all
the time and no damn fun and she hardly
blames them, the happy few, they need
the presence of an absence. She carries
her carapace, the weight of the self-
protected, but dreams she shatters the pear
and the Ford and Bonnie and Clyde and each round
hole through metal and flesh, each round-eyed
hole is splatting *me*, *me*, the word *me*!

Cramps

1.

He'd love to teach his cat a tune:
pure poetry at last! He planned
to raise cathedrals, noble erections . . .
instead explains how all the buttresses
keep flying off
in the wrong directions.

Why is it God,
otherwise gifted,
Who made the horse to laugh, ha, ha,
in the battle, why couldn't God, Who plucked
Leviathan out with a hook, spare him
a tittle or jot
more talent?

2.

Belly-clutched, he feels he's getting
iceage of the heart, or going
sane beyond repair, and life
takes silence for consent.

                        At times,
alone, on his own, he'd trade both hands
for a single clap of applause.

Not Seeing the Sea

Climbing the dunes—not seeing the sea—
I pause to hear the rush and boom,
hiss and rush of the breakers, sound
as of 12,000 women scrubbing bloody
chainmail.
        In my thought, between
two waves, I strike it done, dumb;
a hush: not day: not night. So much
for history. The wild field gleams.

Declare a silence, brutal years.

'Who Then Is Crazy?'

At evening I pause, neglected pen
in hand like a miniature fasces, eyes
revealing a hurt no calm nor healthy
children nor even guiltless sleep
can heal, for look, the crazies run
in the streets, they gnaw
their nails for blood . . .

I think it is their pain for which
I yearn—who then is crazy?—feeling
nothing, the horror
of feeling nothing,
they fuck for their lives
in heatless rooms.

14

The Evidence

My friends away, I feed their cats,
who lean against my legs, pass,
repass, mrrrr through a silence dense
as cold, unqualified cold, though this
is a summer day where I go my rounds
with the blue tin watering can, serving
the fiddleleaf ficus, the octopus tree.

Finished, oddly awed, the key
light in my hand on its poppit chain,
I pause, wait: above the clarified
kitchen sink, across the length
of linoleum, out beyond the lawn
in the meadow the purple loosestrife blazes,
ordered and mad at once, and I am

witness to the evidence
of choice: chairs; a napkin holder;
magazines that came and came;
notes held up by the phone with paint-chipped
magnets; yellow, blue, alphabet
letters on the fridge that spell
confusion in Finno-Ugric; children's

paintings tacked to the doors; rooms
a child no longer a child will remember—
clutter to bear familiar pain
to the heart: the smell of one's parents; photos
in silver frames on the polished dresser;
monogrammed backs of brushes; cuff links . . .
the unrelenting, historical air.

My Old Professor in a Bar

I saw him twice dead drunk, once
in a silence so pure I thought of the gulls
who stand so still on the winter Charles
you'd think their soles were frozen flat.
And the other time he sang, explained
that he'd lived his life as if behind
a waterfall, awed by the torrent, perished
with thirst but unwilling to risk it, going
through everything at last, except
by the inches, dimed to death, showing
a fine regard for black Jack Daniel's,
slowly becoming a Mason jar
for homecured liver pickle; making
a Roman grace of solitude;
for he knows it's death he wakes and wipes
each morning, takes to the movies, sings through,
prays with, almost
drowns, each time . . .
which is why he'll pull that drunken face
no moth would kiss, or treat himself
like eggs he's doomed to walk on, keeping
lone, whole, in search of better
billing than dissolution, a higher
bidder, a fairer
shake.

My Teacher

1.

'Consider this pig,' my teacher said.
'It grows so fat, it smells so bad,
it is perfect of its kind. You must
be brave, express the thoughts you've kept
hidden in your heart, whether joyous
or vile!'

I gave her a page smeared thick
with mud.

'Now this is fine,' she said,
'a poem in praise of wind and bird
for their scattering of seed.'

2.

'I am like a man . . .' I began to explain.

'True,' she said.

'But I yearn to become
a master, a survivor!'

'Too much
trying.'

'I'll try not to try . . .'

'*Much* too much trying!'

3.

'Consider yourself,' she told me, 'you wish
to be loved, admired, for fear of displeasing
you live an endless discipleship
wearing this mask with a grin, constant
but cold.'

'It is my face,' I said.

'May it melt in the sun,' said my teacher.

Borges in Cambridge

'You find this photo flatters me?
Too dark, I think. Too somber. I've sought
throughout my life the Jewish forebear
it's certain I must have. Ur-kafka.
Anything fondly willed may yield
a presence. On well-named Memorial Drive
we chant *The Wanderer* together,
hreran mid hondum hrimcealde sae . . .
I find myself in touch with camps
of the ancients, gone, familiar . . . distant
streets more real than these, hands . . .
you say the gift is *attention?* Exactly:
no more nor less
than a hunting cat's.'

II

Little Song

Feeling abandons claims on you.
Who'll say what your losses mean?
Nobody's one body opens your window.
No one here to touch you clean.

*These are the dark November days
when the English hang themselves.*

Loveknot-weavers slip through loopholes.
Scent aspires to leave the rose.
You, alone, still knit your scruples.
Sands somewhere were the Sphinx's nose.

*These are the dark November days
when the English hang themselves.*

Stone Soup

The magnifying water. The stone
in the white enamel kettle. The cook
begins to tease from the lady, the mean
transported lady, turnipgreen
and bone, to thicken the taste. I can see her
wondering at his shoulder, yielding
a bite of this, a touch of that,
to the miracle soon to come: by God,
between them they're making
soup from a stone,
and he'll eat, he'll smile, he could murder whatever
arranged the story this way: how come
he's always the one who has to start
with charm, charm? Without him, would she
even have the grace to starve?
Who gave *her* all the turnipgreens?

Teaching the Penguins to Fly

The penguins must have had it once,
some drive and wingspan, back before
they joined up in committees to waddle
on slow-moving ice floes, flapping rhetorical
vans. My daughter's first ambition
was teaching them to fly, and she hasn't
forgotten: a poster of Emperor penguins
hangs on her bedroom wall where Beatles
still remain, and Aquarius,
her sign—the fuzzy young and vaguely
gazing adults, all of them look
like kids who've lost their expedition
leader. Emperors. Most of them show
color enough at the neck for the mythseeking
eye to propose, from vestigial yellows,
ancestor roc-macaws. Fifteen,
already the culture-heroine knows
it's nothing like easy to start them moving;
she'll leap and flap her arms to teach
the huge idea: up on the toes,
higher, higher, lift those wings!—
trials down ice-slicked runways, lengthy
political sessions, building the Movement,
until the strongest risk the winter
sky, shedding their dickies, becoming
through generations enormous budgies
who sing in the jungle, in general bird,
the epic tale of the odd liberator
in shirt and jeans who beat the air
with her arms, who sang them
Woody Guthrie, who
brought the revolution
uncramping their lives.

Administrator's Poem

Matched with a bouncy placer swooshing them
over the net from an endless store,
you're bound to be buried, sliding, odd ones
dropped by airlift, flying elephants
based in the boondock backcourts, piling
up no matter how click your serve
or smash your reply, *thwang, thwong,*
this is becoming
a hard-hat job . . .
should you smile for the crowd, and eat a few?
pop some in your pockets? pause to
juggle them nicely? cart some home
to thin the traffic?—now it's raining
mini-pellets, seeded players
fruit and multiply, you yearn
for a Western's cavalry trumpet, but even
if teams of sweepers came they'd be most likely
mounted on high-strung polo ponies,
chipping one out for every two fresh
supplied—a thousand-set game, they're switching
the arc-lights on . . . there's honor . . . a pension . . .
what can one say? weekends . . .
August free . . .

John Berryman

Wry in the councils of judgment he sits
with memorized kings, this prince of care
so fond he stood night sentry here,
wracked by the woodland's green illusion
aspect of gas in a pomp of roses,
a teacher touched by braver days.

Remember him hurting with Crane, Jarrell,
huffing with Hemingway, choosing with Frost
the path less travelled, learning to weep
and swank and swear while dancing the Grand
Fantastic, the Master
of Mistress Bradstreet.

He sang his ardent, snuffed-out friends,
took his clinical turn with finetooth
and howitzer, raging clean of dread.
And he loved up the leaves of the weeds of our wacky
language, did us definitive work
cleaving the spirit's obsidian.

2.

A feeling man, a party to lost
connections, his interests the life of Christ:
Shakespeare's: his own: the pause of all
as a girl begins
to take off her clothes,
he soothed his fey and raucous friends,

always the slouch of style, always
Apollo's languid enterprise;
and flamed his nest, sick phoenix. 'Apparently
left no note,' said the *Times* obit,
but he did, lifelong, in parts, with riffs
and hautbois: literal war on the heart.

In mankind mired and much benighted
he stretched his hand to us mostways,
then *scat*, split, spit, threw his turds
when they came down the corridor for him. He was
a violence passing for song. He blew
o careless love, non serviam.

The Young

They'll learn to doze in silverpoint,
but now they etch, their weapon is
their staring. They despise the prose
all joy's translated in—oh they would
shine, shine as an underground river
flows in darkness, yet is bright
in thought.

The Old

At first it seems there's nobody
not old but you: the bully's 9 feet
tall, six, already goes
to school, oh he is ancient in
his cruelty; the parents live
forever; uncles let you watch
gin rummy, blitz, schneider, aunts
arrive with furs and gossip, cheeks
so lovely cool to kiss and you are
something else who'd understand
their pleasures—what a lesson, watching
Cousin Lou at twenty put
his feet up, trying not to grin
as he contemplates the first fine ash
of his White Owl! You have learned the names
of radio stations, KYW,
WFIL, the price
of an eighth of a pound of lox for breakfast
around the corner on Rockland Street,
but you think of the old as a species, speaking
pidgen to their hearing aids,
the ones who hobble, the ones who smile
to themselves, the ones who pee their pants,
and you by now a lover, father,
bowling with your son, having
your eyes examined, jogging your lungs
eight minutes every morning they're blurring
the changes of season you're getting Sup-hose
and a porkpie hat for Christmas, every
year through thicker glass until you're
moving toward a central light
from which the young are shadows; simply
flutter; less
than real.

The Dream Burglar

Here in an unlocked house I find
a pregnant woman . . . her sleep is filled
with the squirming weight of the future, who
could bear to lift her dream? or even
the dreaming, in the next room,
of the little daughter: already *she* looks
like somebody's sister; they've told her, once
they bring It home, she'll get to hold It,
love It, love It, oh so gently!

The husband in his dream is crabbing,
just as he did with his father years
gone by. He waits for a claw, to take
the joint of oxtail tied to his rope,
the stubborn claw locked as he hauls it
deftly toward the net in a rowboat
among the water hyacinths
on the St. Johns river. Something nudges.
A crab? a tangle of flower roots?
He waits. He will not draw it in.

Beside him, her swollen belly seems,
covered by the sheet, a sacred
mound, or totem
of the tribe.
She smiles . . . I've arrived, in a stranger's room,
so I reach into her dream, I'm fiercely
grabbing on, stealing her blind;
stealing her vision, blind.

Tombstones & Flourishes
for X. J. Kennedy

I treated the whore of life like a lady
and she, she screwed me
properly.

I think the changeless
single thought
of a stone.

Head: hands: gut: phallus:
abdicated
pleasure palace.

Stranger, believe it,
gravity can't
turn the pages.

Now time continues, painstakingly,
meticulous artist,
finishing me.

Hard on the camel,
but think of the eye
of the needle!

Recalling Mr. Frost
for Nick and Eva Linfield

A dauntless taper on a Christmas tree
where apples hang with old world stars of straw
brings Mr. Frost to mind—his blazonry—
for though the other wicks give up to smoke
this last grows strong as if to tease the law
we alter by, and challenging its gist
burns on and on: the flicker of a joke
in favor of presuming to persist.

No miracles seem likely in our day;
no dove-fire eloquence or shaken flow
of flame tongues. Some achieve a wry display
burning for meaning bravely as they go
out to the dark that waits beyond each door
as if to tell us what a light is for.

III

Once the World's On Again

Once the world's on again, goodwife will rise
and groggily fill the coffee pot,
while goodman, a dream running back of his eyes
that he's urging along to its fade-out shot

will stir to the scent of the coffee done,
will yawn half-alive to the torrent of light
as the blinds are unbiased to let in the sun.
What amends for impossible hopes in the night?

She'll ply him with coffee; the newscasters start
a civilization again in his brain,
and the tenure of breathing sends strength to his heart
till he's ready to think of the shuffle and strain

of his day, though his day must surely fail.
For the moment there's comfort: as if a friend
arrived with sunshine, and cheering mail.
After the dreaming, world without end.

'Foolfish'

Princely, his edges undulant,
he couldn't care less what they call him, but somebody
found a joke or a touch of Myshkin
sadness here in the downright style
of the filefish, so he's labeled 'Foolfish'
out of his habit of hovering upside
down in his tank for hours, slim
and dimity white, at home in these waters,
flairing his ruffs like Elizabeth;
no more compelled or odd in his ways
than an astronaut, or the moon.

Globed Thistles

Like nobles by the path they stand—
the king will come, and look like them,
these tall, blue-headed thistles, being
exactly who they are, a splendor
of hardihood, unwillingness
to bend or please or pass as a soft-petaled
saint of the fields and hollows. Reach
the england of your settled years,
your sun and moon in their traces, still
these garish highland hedgehogs are
your cousins, fierce in their fiber, hearts-
of-fire that rise slim-stalked to stare
their sister sun, the very sun
in the face—a pride
of thistles.

The Legend of Kuan Yin

The icons show her, male, female,
many-armed. The legend goes
that wanting force, she swore a vow:
*May my body crack the day I fail
a single needy person!* Of course,
she failed, and in her brokenness
became herself; for from the thousand
fissures where her very body
cracked by willing mercy grew
the thousand arms
and thousand hands
of compassion.

Before a Statue of Kuan Yin

sufficient to the burning
that it burn

the light sufficient
to the length of day

our hope in how our hopes endure
beyond all promise
of a cure

In the Forties

you give up wasting your youth, move on
to the wasting of the rest . . . at times
you notice a sultry, weathered feeling,
as if your thoughts had spent a week
in a sherry cask, or your life's a house
where the unpainted shingles have darkened at last
from sea salt. Think 'Gray is beautiful,'
and a strolling girl on the beach may give you
a look—something to do with her father?
his smile, his military brushes?—
that proves you're still yourself, for time
begins beyond your gates, another's
vision counts you down but not
your own: within, you're going for extra
bases, running towards waves, strolling
through sunlight, pigeons, traffic, anyone,
anyone you see
liable to change you.

Comparing X-Rays

The brute, intense congruity
of ribs upon each spinal tree . . .

stranger, lover, this we share,
everything but threadbare

flesh. Our lips are quick, but jaws
take firmer hold on natural laws.

Trapped within this hopeless maze,
our lives will lose their separate ways.

Variation on a Theme From Horace

Out from Bedlam on the train
that clackets him to boxer pup,
to patio to entertain,
to sleep to struggle to wake up,

he finds a greener climate yields
a charm the city can't provide;
his foreign shore across the fields
the wife-filled car at stationside.

Spider

Between two pines she hangs mouth-high
(she's having lunch sent in) until I
puff to see her move, my wind
her ration. Once she's widely swayed
she rows out to inspect her nets,
where she, before the Lord of Flies
came by, sat calm. She scuttles back,
and gives a twitch to tense the web,
but now each time I blow she fails
to budge: her silk philosophy's
intact, and as for teasing, that's
my problem. Though I make it swing,
the cosmos that her guts have spun
still holds. We end our meeting
in a standoff.

To a Lady

Dear lady, by your fingertips
you rhyme me to a feather.
I run the rapids of your arms
from here to Minnesota.
You sun me bright, you sigh me on
till half of Iceland's burning.
I bless you for your leafy ways.
My breath be all you're wearing.

Song of the Scholar of Love

My colleagues chart tomorrow's weather;
contemplate the shape of space;
reconstruct from bone and feather
species fallen out of grace;
for natural scholars earn their bread
with braincells densely tenanted . . .
but I'm forgetting altogether
every queen that Henry wed,

Iseult, Francesca, what's-her-name,
the girl who sighed 'I swan' to Zeus—
the lore of love, the field I claim
(where ignorance is no excuse)
goes dim—that Greeks and Trojans died,
that Cressid either loved or lied,
I know, or did . . . your smile's to blame,
where all research is satisfied.

Found Art

The leaves along the walk were pressed
to concrete. You could hang a slab.
Dimmed of brightness, deeply held
like negatives of color-prints,
these echoes of a greener saying:
brilliant, stone-stained ghosts.

Essential Praises of Silence

1.

A faithless body-builder, wanting
the moon but not the leaping, sick
of the sweat for salt, the
furnace wheels, the
creak of impossible
loads, how
may a man raise up his head much less
his voice these days? Only the suicides
('Days? What days?') only the suicides
answer.

2.

I brought my hurt to Love, but Love
was busy, phone
off the hook . . . so I whispered
my purpose to the Brave, but the Brave
were enjoying themselves in the mirrors, so
I paused at the house of Thought: nobody
home, and at last I carried myself
to Sleep, who offers, with hammer and nails,
to fix me up
with his beautiful Sister.

44

3.

Again then again I catch myself
in these stitches of my breath to sing
essential praises of silence until
the song becomes, through a grace beyond
my calling a song
of clanging day
that cures the peace
of night, a song
of rising that leans against the stone
that blocks the cave of my life.

After the 'I Ching'

Abrupt as it is with fire, with death;
a wind appears, and grasses bend.
Of three men walking, two lose breath;
but one man, walking, finds his friend.

Chung Fu moves even pigs and fishes:
unblinking eye: sincerity.
One fords the stream; one sifts the ashes;
one utters the groans of a man of eighty.

Beneficence: to feed on air.
To son and man the same advice:
with instruments of earthenware
to make the vernal sacrifice

while grasses turn in the wind;
while all the grasses bend.

On a Jaina Miniature

The dawning world's a wave between two trees
that yearn in form and color toward the sun.

So we too have beginning as our nature,
who move through tides of absence like the light.

Courting Surfaces

To court these surfaces
unscathed, to pass over fiery rocks
or slide down an oily pane or walk
the waters, tension held, requires
a lightness, speed, yearning, the danger's
to stop, look down, attend until you
deepen, disappear, an aspect
of where you are, at one with its hue
and weather, weight and changing, as a
seed will die, become the thrust
of tendril, root, and bloom, a native
fully held in time, someone
here—here or nowhere—all along.